PRAISE FOR
CLASSROOM MANAGEMENT IN THE DIGITAL AGE

"I have had the pleasure of collaborating and leading with Patrick and Heather on several growth and change initiatives associated with teaching in a digital age. This book represents the thoughtful and practical ideas they use to support professional development of teachers and student learning. In an environment where electronic tools offer incredible opportunity and potential distraction, this will prove to be a go-to resource for new and experienced teachers as they seek to harness the power of a digital-rich classroom."

—**Devin Pratt**, Assistant Head of School at Frankfurt International School

"From two leading practitioners with firsthand experience, Heather Dowd and Patrick Green's book is a rich resource and reference point for educators engaging with mobile technology in a 1:1 environment. *Classroom Management in the Digital Age* is full of concrete, actionable strategies ensuring student-centered collaborative learning is at the center of the mobile device experience."

—**John Mikton**, Director of e-Learning at Inter-Community School Zurich

"*Classroom Management in the Digital Age* is a perfect addition to any 1:1 implementation plan. It is something I would definitely include in my IT/EdTech Roadmap process and hand out to teachers before adding more devices to their classroom. Heather and Patrick have written an easy-to-follow step-by-step guide for today's teachers and schools acknowledging the concept of 'New Approaches for New Tools.' Well done!"

—**Mike Pelletier**, EdTech Consultant

"Heather Dowd and Patrick Green's *Classroom Management in the Digital Age* will make a significant contribution to the teaching and learning strategies employed by teachers in schools. The authors bring their extensive knowledge and experience as educators to the added layer of tech implementation and device usage. Not surprisingly, the advice and strategies they provide are based on sound educational principles and common sense.

"What sets this book apart is that they acknowledge the importance of partnering with parents so that there is a consistency in terms of expectations of behavior and usage and the reinforcement of them in the home. The authors also outline the benefits and methodologies for collaboration, sharing devices and extension opportunities as well as what may be considered basic but in reality are significant skills and knowledge. They address the importance of developing students who engage with technology in safe, smart, respectful, and responsible ways and the most appropriate resource for explicitly addressing the key concepts of digital citizenship. Educators are always on the lookout for treasures to enhance their teaching; this one is gold!"

—*Robyn Treyvaud*, Founder, Cyber Safe Kids

"Balance is essential. Taking us through the reasons behind our choices to use or set technology aside, Heather and Patrick show both veteran and new teachers a toolkit of tips and tricks that are very easy to add to your routines. My mentor once advised that the best indicator of a successful teaching day is leaving the building with the kids more worn out than you are. If trying to figure out how to manage the devices in your room leaves you frustrated (or if you just need a few new resources to up your game), read this book."

—*Rebecca R. Clark*, middle school teacher and Google Certified Innovator

"In *Classroom Management in the Digital Age*, Heather Dowd and Patrick Green are able to translate their own expert classroom practices into an easy-to-understand guide for teachers in a technology-enriched classroom and school. Whether you are just getting started or are a veteran teacher, this book can help you to become more effective in the twenty-first-century classroom."

—*Clint Hamada*, Educational Technology Coordinator, International School of Beijing and Founding Partner, Eduro Learning

CLASSROOM
MANAGEMENT
IN THE
DIGITAL AGE

HEATHER DOWD AND PATRICK GREEN

These books are available at special discounts when purchased in quantity for use as premiums, promotions, fundraising, and educational use. For inquiries and details, contact the publisher: edtechteam.com/press.

Published by EDTechTeam Press
Editing and Interior Design by My Writers' Connection
Cover by Genesis Kohler

Library of Congress Control Number: 2016949995
Paperback ISBN: 978-1-945167-12-6
eBook ISBN: 978-1-945167-13-3

Irvine, California

FOR DOUG AND BECKY

Contents

Preface

Why You Need This Book

Some schools have used devices in classrooms for a number of years; however, we suspect the technology-equipped classroom is new and potentially uncomfortable territory for many of you. And while a connected classroom provides powerful learning opportunities, it also brings new challenges. *Classroom Management in the Digital Age* will help you transfer your current classroom management strategies to a new classroom where every student is connected and help you deal with new challenges in a positive and productive way.

Many teachers are confident in their teaching, but less so with technology, creating anxiety around their ability to adapt to the changing education landscape. This book will remind seasoned educators there are many tried-and-true practices on which they can continue to rely, while also offering tips and tricks to deal with the nuances of technology-rich classrooms.

Types of Devices

Increasingly, twenty-first-century classrooms have a one-to-one (1:1) student to Internet-connected-device ratio. Currently, a variety of 1:1 device programs are found in schools around the world. Macbooks, Windows, Chromebooks laptop programs, and iPad and Android tablet programs are the most popular. At times we will discuss details about tablets or laptops; however, because there are so many platforms available, and technology is constantly changing, most often we will use the generic term "device" which can be read as the specific device each student is using.

Many schools have invested in Learning Management Systems (LMS) to deliver curriculum online or, more often, to augment face-to-face classes with digital tools and other components. Some popular LMS are Moodle, Blackboard, Hapara Teacher Dashboard, Schoology, Google Classroom, Haiku, Edmodo, and Canvas. While we do not venture specifically into any one LMS, we do reference them generally as they tend to have many of the same functionalities. Ask if your school has an LMS you could take advantage of to enhance your use of devices with students.

A VARIETY OF 1:1 SETUPS

Along with the 1:1 student-to-device ratio comes a variety of setup options. The first differentiator, of course, is the type of device to be used, typically a laptop or tablet, and the operating system. Another consideration is the ownership model. Will the devices be owned by the school or by families? Adding more layers of complexity are whether or not the devices are uniform, how the devices are deployed, and whether they are checked out to individual students or to classrooms to be used as shared devices. Additionally, your students' ages may determine which 1:1 program is appropriate.

While we have opinions about preferred 1:1 program models, we have tried to write generically for all situations.

HOW TO READ THIS BOOK

Classroom Management in the Digital Age contains four main sections:

Classroom Procedures

Classroom Rules and Expectations

Teaching Tips and Strategies

Partnering with Parents

Feel free to use the table of contents to find the information you need when you need it. We expect and encourage you to "cherry pick" the resources and ideas you need as you set up your 1:1 classroom.

Classroom Procedures

This chapter includes processes and procedures you can use to ensure your classroom runs smoothly and efficiently. You will need to teach these procedures to students and give them a chance to practice. Soon, the procedures will happen naturally without a word from you.

Classroom Rules and Expectations

This chapter includes advice about rules you may want to enforce in your classroom regarding technology. It also includes some rules we have seen other teachers use which you may want to consider.

Teaching Tips and Strategies

This chapter includes strategies you can use in your teaching practice as you plan the learning activities. These strategies, used by you, help create a well-managed classroom.

Partnering with Parents

This chapter includes ideas for communicating with parents about your 1:1 classroom. While your school may have its own plan for communicating with parents, it is also a good idea for you to engage in direct communication. By partnering with parents about the expectations you have in your classroom, you empower parents to reinforce these expectations at home.

Although we wrote this book for educators working directly with students in the classroom, we also include some helpful resources related to setting up a 1:1 device program at a school. However, this book is not meant to be a guide to setting up a 1:1 device program. It is intended to be a guide for teachers in a 1:1 setting.

INTRODUCTION

Times have changed. Classrooms once featuring paper, pencils, and textbooks as the main teaching resources have evolved into spaces where each student can hold a device in his hands allowing him to download more information than a physical library can hold. Students can connect and collaborate globally with peers and experts while creating presentations, works of art, music, and video with the same tools used by professionals. The addition of digital devices has given our students amazing access to information and nearly endless creative opportunities.

While our classrooms and the resources they hold have changed dramatically over the years, our students' needs are still very much the same. Our students need caring teachers who provide safe environments for taking risks and learning from mistakes. They need teachers who have high expectations and who challenge students to rise to meet those expectations. Students also need clear boundaries and other support structures to help them succeed. Effective teachers create this type of classroom culture where students are free to be the best learners they can be.

DISCIPLINE

THIS BOOK IS NOT ABOUT DISCIPLINE

Let's be clear: This book is NOT about discipline, and it will not give any tips on creating or implementing a discipline plan. We have not omitted this because we think you don't need one. Of course you do. Inevitably, you will have a student who misbehaves, and a discipline plan will help you deal with the misconduct effectively; however, there are plenty of other discipline books—and classroom management books. Our aim is to help you set up your device-rich classrooms in a way that maximizes learning and minimizes confusion, disruption, and discipline issues.

THE BEST DISCIPLINE PLAN IS A SCHOOL-WIDE PLAN

While this book is not about discipline specifically, there are a couple of important things to note: First, when it comes to discipline plans, a coordinated school-wide policy is much more effective than individual classroom plans. These plans make it easier for students to know the rules and consequences; they also make it easier for teachers to know the rules and enforce them. If your school does not have a school-wide discipline plan that is inclusive of technology-related infractions, prod your principal to start investigating one. Everyone will benefit.

DON'T TAKE AWAY THE LEARNING TOOL

The second thing to note about discipline is that taking a device away from a student is not really an option for a consequence. At the least, it should be used only as a last resort. Remember, we have devices in our classrooms because they are powerful learning tools. If our job is to help students learn, taking away a learning tool is counterproductive. Consider this illustration from pre-device days:

> *Students are assigned to write a paragraph, and most students are completing the assignment. But Johnny has written a note to his friend across the room and starts to pass it when he looks up and makes eye contact with the teacher.*

In this example, if the teacher takes away the pencil and paper because Johnny used them inappropriately, he will not be able to complete the paragraph writing. So the teacher needs to deal with the behavior and direct the student to get back on task and use the tools appropriately.

The same is true in today's classroom when a student is misusing his or her device. The behavior must be dealt with, but the student must still be able to use the tool to complete the task. This is even more imperative today, as teachers have the collective responsibility to teach the content of our disciplines, develop good digital citizens, and prepare our students for their futures.

CLASSROOM PROCEDURES

THE TERMS *PROCEDURES* AND *ROUTINES* ARE OFTEN USED INTERCHANGEABLY IN EDUCATION CIRCLES. Typically, they refer to processes used frequently in a classroom to accomplish tasks in the way the teacher prefers. Well-defined classroom procedures use time efficiently and, therefore, allow more time for learning. Additionally, procedures decrease misbehavior and disruptions in class since students are less likely to be disruptive when expectations are clear.

Teachers who establish procedures for common classroom tasks enjoy a more smoothly running class than those who do not. Adding the complexity of digital devices to a classroom increases the importance of having clear processes and procedures in place.

TEACHING PROCEDURES

Students learn by doing. You can't just tell them how to do something and expect they have learned it. This is why there are so many other instructional strategies beyond lecturing. The same is true about procedures. They must be taught, practiced, and reinforced—not just stated once. The following four steps will help ensure your procedures are both clear to and mastered by your students.

Step One: Teach the Procedure—Teachers should clearly articulate and demonstrate the procedure to the students while also explaining why they want things done a specific way.

Step Two: Practice—Students practice the procedure as the teachers directed.

Step Three: Monitor, Correct, and Reinforce—Teachers should monitor the students as they practice the procedure, offering feedback in the form of correction or reinforcement.

Step Four: Review—Students will be quick to learn most procedures but may not always remember to use them in your classes. Teachers need to review procedures throughout the school year as a reminder. Take time to review procedures when necessary; the time spent will be worth it.

Many of our students juggle multiple classrooms and a variety of teachers with varying degrees of reliance on procedures. What might seem like logical and simple processes to your adult brain can be just another set of rules to a student. Remember that digital devices are common in our students' lives. Often students use these devices with little supervision or set expectations. Assume that students have good intentions and review procedures when necessary.

Consider posting certain procedures on the wall for easy reference, or consider making a visual to help students remember how things are done in your classroom. These can help shift the responsibility of following procedures to the students.

HEADS UP! CALLING STUDENTS TO ATTENTION

If you are talking over your students, they are not listening. This was true before devices were in your classroom, and it is still true. When teachers are talking, students should be actively listening, which means they are not talking and they are not using a device.

> When teachers are talking, students should be actively listening, which means they are not talking and they are not using a device.

One of the first things you learned is to demand your students' attention before giving direct instructions. This is even more important in a device-rich classroom where you are competing for attention, not just with friends and textbooks, but with a myriad of engaging websites, apps, and social media. Whether you ring a bell, count backwards from five, or use a clapping sequence the students repeat, you need a clear signal for students to redirect their attention to you. Additionally, you need to set clear expectations for how the students will come to attention in your classroom.

EXPECTATIONS FOR ATTENTION

EYES ON THE TEACHER

Eye contact is one of the most important components of active listening. Students are not listening to the teacher if they are not looking at the teacher. Students may claim to be great multi-taskers, but they simply are not able to completely focus on two things at once. And a teacher's voice cannot compete with rich images, video, text, or audio coming from a screen—let alone an engaging activity you have set students to work on. Do not start speaking until you have eye contact with your students.

HANDS OFF THE DEVICE

Students need to have their hands off their devices. While younger students may need something specific to do with their hands, the point is to separate students from their devices. This decreases the temptation to become quickly immersed in what they were previously doing if they happen to lose eye contact with the teacher.

SCREENS NOT VISIBLE TO THE STUDENT

To further increase the potential for students to stay attentive, device screens need to be out of eyesight of students. Students can close the lids of laptops or put them at a 45-degree angle. iPads can be set screen-down on the desk. By physically removing the screen from their vision, students are able to more easily switch their attention to the teacher and not be drawn back quickly by something flashing on the screen.

EARBUDS OUT OF EARS

If students are engaged in an activity requiring earbuds or headphones, students need to remove them so they can focus on the teacher's instruction.

SIGNAL

While the expectations for attention are pretty universal, signaling for attention is much more personal. Very likely you can adapt a strategy you used in your classroom before devices were introduced. Or perhaps you will want to try one of the crowd-sourced strategies shared below. Either way, find a workable strategy and use it consistently so student response becomes routine. Getting this right will save lots of class time otherwise wasted on battling to capture the attention of your students.

PRACTICE THE SIGNAL

Once you decide which strategies are going to work for you, give students a chance to practice them at the beginning of the school year. If you select a signal to indicate students should close their devices and look up, practice it regularly during the first few times students are using devices. Practicing will make it second nature for you and your students.

SIGNAL IDEAS

Patrick likes to be very direct in his laptop classes by loudly stating, "Forty-five your screens!" This signals for attention while reminding his students of the expectation to put their screen at an angle so they will not be distracted while he gives further instructions. Other teachers have shared their favorite signals below.

"To avoid students closing one device only to pull out their phone, we started saying 'de-screen' during times of direct instruction. The idea was to get kids off all screens—not just their laptops." —*Jon Corrippo*

"In my classes, I use the term 'tip the top' to signal students to put their screens in a position out of their view." —*Joan Brown*

"Calling out, 'Dock it!' works well in districts where students can use their mobile devices. 'Dock it' means students need to put their device in the upper-left corner of the desk. During 'dock it' time, students are not to touch their mobile devices." —*Christopher Kavcak*

"I very softly say, 'If you can hear me, clap your hands once. If you can hear me, clap your hands twice...' and so on. They need to stop typing, reading, and engaging in all activity related to the device. Students usually comply before the sixth clap." —*Pablo Luis Castillo*

"With younger students, I set a three-second challenge. When I say, 'screens off, looking this way,' they have three seconds to comply. It's important to warn them so they are prepared to stop (e.g., 'Three-second challenge coming soon.') After I call the signal, I look at my watch. The students usually take ten to fifteen seconds to comply—which for me is a result! You could also give a reward to the class if every student achieves the goal of three seconds."
—*Graham Bowman*

"I call out 'Screen forward!' and my students turn their screens to face me. This way I can quickly see where they are on an assignment and give additional instructions without distraction."
—*Cari Wilson*

COLLECTING STUDENT WORK

Before digital devices entered our classrooms, students physically handed in their assignments. Teachers of well-managed classrooms trained their students in the routines of passing in papers or putting them into a specific bin. I taught students to pass papers to the side (to avoid hitting the person in front of them with a pile of papers). Then one student walked down the last aisle and collected each row's pile and collated them for me. Technology makes this process a bit more complex. While some of our digital tools make collecting student work easier, the wide range of media we assign students to use actually creates the need for multiple methods.

A DIGITAL DROP BOX

Teachers need a default location to collect digital assignments. A digital drop box, or folder, is a great choice because this online space is accessible to both students and teachers, and most drop boxes accept multiple file types including documents, slide decks, images, etc. Many Learning Management Systems (LMS) have a built-in drop box feature with varied functionality. This flexibility makes it the best default system.

One of the best uses of technology in education, however, is the ability for students to publish to a wider audience. In many cases, publishing the final product is a more authentic means of submission than handing it in to the teacher. Student blogs or shared documents are great publishing tools.

STUDENT BLOGS

Teachers can use student blogs to collect kids' work by considering the assignment "submitted" when it is posted. While written essays are an obvious item to publish on a blog, student-created videos or still images (e.g., poster or infographic) can also be posted. LMS features or setting up a feed reader can make visiting student blogs as easy for the teacher as accessing a digital drop box.

SHARED DOCUMENT OR SPREADSHEET WITH LINKS TO PROJECTS

A shared document or spreadsheet where students can drop in links to their final products sometimes makes the most sense for collecting assignments. Say your students are creating short documentaries about the American Civil Rights Movement. Collecting gigabytes of video files doesn't make sense when uploading them to YouTube is free. Students can upload their videos to YouTube and copy the link to the shared document. This also allows students to share their work with parents and other interested parties and gives students access to each other's projects for peer reviews. Finally, because you will be proud of the amazing work your students have created, you will have a ready-made list of links to share with other members of your community.

Even in a device-rich classroom, you will likely still have students turning in some physical products such as a printed essay or hand-drawn mind-map. You may still need a pass-your-papers-to-the-teacher process, but keep in mind that students can digitize analog assignments by taking a photo and adding it to their blog or turning it in digitally.

Students can digitize analog assignments by taking a photo and adding it to their blog or turning it in digitally.

Because students can creatively show their learning in various ways, both on paper and digitally, you will likely need a default way to collect both types of work. You have a variety of products with multiple collection strategies available to you. The most important thing is to communicate clearly about how each assignment will be turned in or published.

COMMUNICATING THE DAY'S AGENDA AND HOMEWORK

As we stated earlier, good teaching practices before devices were in classrooms are still good practices today. One of those practices is posting learning objectives as well as the day's agenda and homework. This communicates to students what they are going to learn and how they are going to learn it. Posting the learning objectives and class activities in a visible place minimizes confusion and maximizes time learning.

CONSISTENT AND IMMEDIATE

Students should not have to work hard to figure out what is going on in a teacher's classroom. Information should be easy for students to find, which means teacher consistency is paramount. Students should find the agenda, homework, and objectives in the same location and in the same format each day. They should always be able to see it as they walk into class so they are not left waiting or wondering when it will be revealed.

DIGITAL OR ANALOG?

The benefits of posting agendas and homework digitally are numerous:

- Students can access online information 24/7.
- Links to supplemental resources and materials students need for activities can enrich the information.
- Teachers can allow parents access to online information.
- Students can access information they missed when absent, even before they return to school.

While these benefits are all positive, you might consider also posting an abbreviated version of the agenda and homework on the whiteboard or on a flip chart. An analog version gives you one location to use when you want to bring everyone's attention back from their screens during the course of the class.

EXAMPLES AND POSSIBLE TOOLS

As long as students know how to access the information, nearly any digital space will work for posting agendas, homework, and lessons. If your school uses an LMS (Moodle, Google Classroom, Blackboard, Schoology, Canvas, Haiku, etc.), posting your agenda and homework on it is best so your students have one place to access all of their information across multiple courses. Another option is to use a slide deck, such as Google Presentations or Microsoft PowerPoint, where you add a new slide for each day. The deck of slides is available online so students can access it outside the classroom.

An online calendaring system, such as Google Calendar, is another viable option and has the added bonus of integrating with mobile devices. Using a productivity tool like a calendar can help students learn skills such as making to-do lists for large projects.

HEATHER'S STORY

Before my students had their own devices in the classroom, the lesson plans I wrote, either on paper or in a digital document, were meant for me. I did not share my lesson-planning document with students. For my students, I rewrote the learning objectives, class agenda, and homework in my classroom—quite the chore since I taught multiple subjects in one day.

When my school introduced a 1:1 laptop program and my students all had a device, many of my former routines changed. Because technology was readily available in my classroom and it became easy to put information online with free, easy publishing tools (blogs and websites), I began to put class objectives and agendas online.

As I transitioned to online class information, I started using the online site as my lesson planner rather than maintaining a separate document for myself. As I planned units, I put links to the activities and resources directly onto my class site. Having my lessons online is convenient and efficient, and I never have to answer, "What did we do yesterday?" when someone is absent. Similarly, there is never a reason for a student to say, "Are we doing anything today?"

My class site has become my lesson planner and the place my students go for the class calendar, including objectives, activities, and homework. They bookmark the site for easy access any time they need it. Plus, I can project the needed information at the beginning of every class instead of spending extra time copying the objectives and agenda to another location for students.

ACTIVATOR: WHAT STUDENTS DO WHEN THEY WALK INTO THE ROOM

Teachers of well-managed classrooms often utilize a special activity to begin class. Whether you call this activity a warm-up, an activator, a bell-ringer, or a sponge (soak up every minute), the goal is to get the class started on time without the teacher needing to give explicit instructions. The pedagogical theory is these activities (short, pre-thinking, pre-reading, problem solving, or journaling exercises) help students transition into the subject being taught. They also free up the teacher to attend to individual students, take attendance, or address other daily tasks while the students are getting centered and focused on the learning at hand. As with any procedure, students must understand the expectations. The teacher must repeat the expectations a number of times and provide practice opportunities along with consistency both in frequency of use and in location of the instructions.

The same digital tools used for communicating agendas and homework can be used for communicating instructions for an activator. You may want to include the activator and always display it at the start of each class. Susan, a veteran teacher, uses Google Slides to communicate this. The class agenda, including the activator and the homework, is noted each day on one slide. The deck grows by one additional slide each day and becomes a record of class activity. The teacher displays the daily slide on the projector to start each class period and, because the slide deck is shared to the students, they can also access it from home.

The activator instructions should be easily understood by all students. They should include the following:

- instructions for what to do
- an explicit list of tools students are expected to use
- instructions about what students should do with their devices

ACTIVATOR

1. Close all applications except Microsoft Word.

2. Use shapes and lines to construct ten symbols that have a positive connotation.

ACTIVATOR

1. Close your laptops.

2. Take out a piece of paper and a pencil.

3. Draw ten symbols that have a positive connotation.

ATTENDANCE

Taking attendance is a mundane daily task and should be completed quickly, without the attention of the students. If students are actively involved in the attendance procedure or waiting for the teacher to complete it, time for learning is wasted. The most effective way to take attendance is to quickly compare the seating chart with the students present while they are busy with a task. While the addition of Internet-connected devices has changed many aspects of teaching and learning, taking attendance is not one of them. Whether you mark students absent on a piece of paper or in some sort of online system, the goal is to do it quickly and accurately without wasting the students' time.

Once you have a plan for an activator, you can consider options for taking attendance. The activator itself might give you a way to take attendance, or you can use an online quizzing tool. As students log in to the tool and submit answers, the teacher can see who has not submitted an answer and mark the student absent. Sometimes it is also nice to have a handwritten method available; for example, one teacher we know creates a document at the beginning of the school year with a list of all students in the class followed by columns of check boxes. If she cannot access a device and needs to quickly take attendance on paper, she has this document to jot who is absent. Later she can transfer the information to the online system.

ABSENT STUDENTS

Device-rich classrooms and 1:1 programs have made dealing with absent students easier than ever before. Teachers of well-managed classrooms have always had processes and procedures for absent students—typically, handouts and other items the student missed were placed in a folder along with the agendas from the days missed. Today, the agendas and homework, as well as links to any "handouts," should be posted online, making it easy for the absent student to know what she missed before she returns to class. The teacher should not need to post anything extra for an absent student. Rather, the regular communication of the agenda and homework should suffice for both the students in attendance and those who missed class. Absent students may need to meet with the teacher for clarification, and this could be handled while the other students are working on the activator.

Students and teachers must have clear expectations with regard to absences. The teacher's role is to communicate the agendas and homework consistently. The student's role is to review the information before she returns to class and come prepared with any questions for clarification. Together the teacher and the student should agree on a timeline for completing outstanding assignments.

Procedures for Shared Devices

If your classroom has shared devices (more than one student using each device), you will need to consider several elements and set up procedures that will likely be different from those needed in a 1:1 program or when the students have their own personal devices.

Device Accounts

Many devices allow each student to create his own account; for example, a student using a Chromebook can log in to her own account with a username and password and instantly have access to all of her personal files. Laptops using Windows or Mac operating systems also have functionality for multiple users. When this feature is available, use it to keep files and information specific to each student from being tampered with by other students.

Other Internet Accounts

If students are using devices which do not allow for individual device accounts, they will need to log out of any accounts they log in to on the shared device, and you will need to make time in class for this. You must remind students of the importance of protecting their accounts by logging out when they are finished.

WHERE TO SAVE WORK

Another consideration is where students will save their work. The best option is for students to save their work in the cloud in their individual accounts. Google Apps or Microsoft 365 makes this easy, and it can also be done in most LMS. Depending on the devices you have, how they are set up, and whether or not your students have cloud services, you may need to create a workflow for students to save their work on the local device or on a local school network. Perhaps each student could own a folder on the device and put his work there.

EXTENSION OPPORTUNITIES

Teachers of well-managed classrooms always have a plan for dealing with students who complete assigned work early because, in the absence of a plan, students will find something to fill their time, and their activities can potentially distract other students from completing their tasks. In many classrooms, the default activity available to students who complete their tasks has been reading a book of their choosing. This is popular because reading is valued by educators, is an independent task, can be completed quietly, does not distract other students, and does not require any additional management from the teacher.

The addition of digital devices to classrooms has added some complexity to this situation. Digital devices are so powerfully versatile, they literally open a whole world of possible activities. While students can obviously read on their devices, they can also play games, watch videos, compose music, create art, and on and on. The key is for the teacher to harness the power of the device for extension and independent learning, and not let it be a distraction. To accomplish this, the

> Digital devices are so powerfully versatile, they literally open a whole world of possible activities.

teacher of a well-managed classroom must offer students a list of activities from which to choose and clearly communicate expectations.

The worst thing a teacher can do is allow students complete autonomy over their choice of activity. This will lead to a culture of sloppy work, as students will want to complete the task quickly in order to move on to activities of their own choosing (online games, watching pop culture videos, etc.). I advise teachers to give students a few main options which have educational value and can be completed independently. Of course, they could also choose the age-old favorite: read a book.

WORK ON A PORTFOLIO

Online portfolios offer students an opportunity to reflect on their learning and showcase their thinking processes as well as their talents. Because students are continually learning and growing, a portfolio is a work in progress to be continually tweaked and updated with the student's latest work and thinking. By having a portfolio system in place, perhaps a blog, website, or stand-alone software, teachers will always have a place to direct a student who completes an assignment before the rest of the class.

EXTENSION EXERCISES

Extension exercises are activities vetted by the teacher and specific to the class or topic. Games, subject-specific software, WebQuest, and a YouTube playlist are a few examples.

GAMES

Online programs such as Quizlet can be used to create a game using the vocabulary from the current unit of study. In many of these online games, students can work independently while a leaderboard tracks their personal best and allows them to compete with other students.

SUBJECT-SPECIFIC SOFTWARE

Perhaps your school subscribes to an online site or software for independent practice of skills. Many of these programs are available for math, vocabulary, typing, foreign languages, etc. The best programs include a teacher dashboard so you can check on student progress.

WEBQUEST

A WebQuest challenges students to go deeper into a topic. The teacher prepares a set of links to websites for the student to follow, and there is typically a set of questions to keep the student focused.

YOUTUBE PLAYLIST

The teacher creates a playlist of videos students are allowed to view. Again, typically there is a set of questions to keep the student on track.

GENERIC LIST

The generic list of activities can be applied broadly in both self-contained classrooms and subject-specific courses. We have listed three options to help you start thinking about others you could add to this list.

SCREENCAST

Students create a screencast teaching a concept to other students.

DEVELOP A PLAYLIST

Students create a list of the top five YouTube videos related to a current topic of study.

CREATE FLASHCARDS

Students create flashcards or an online game like Quizlet that other students can use to study the current topic.

FILE NAMING CONVENTIONS

When we were students, teachers gave us instructions about where to write our names on our homework: "Put your name, date, and class in the top right corner." Maybe they were trying to teach us to be organized, or perhaps they were just trying to stay sane while grading papers. (It was probably a little of both.) While digital classrooms require fewer papers to be physically printed and turned in, teachers still need a way to know who did what for the purpose of assessing and reporting. Just as you consider how students will turn in work in this new environment (see "Collecting Student Work" section), you need to give students clear instructions about how to name their files or give you links.

> Naming conventions help students get organized and use best practices for saving, and later finding, their work.

Naming conventions help students get organized and use best practices for saving, and later finding, their work. They also help you when you grade assignments. Secondary students might name their files using lastname-firstname-period-assignment while elementary students might simply use firstname-assignment. You know your students and what might work best for their development level.

More and more LMS are developing functionality to allow teachers to create assignments for each student with the press of a button, eliminating the need to teach naming conventions. Typically, these assignments are already organized by class and include the name of the student. The best of these systems gives joint access to the file once it is created so the teacher can periodically check on progress instead of having to wait for the final submission. If your school is using an LMS, it might be worth your time to investigate the assignment-creation functionality.

PRINTING

Having a device in the hands of every student will change your printing needs. In fact, many schools implementing a 1:1 program see a natural reduction in the amount of printing, even if they have not expressly tried to be a paperless school. This happens naturally as teachers share more documents digitally instead of on paper and collect assignments digitally rather than have students print them out. Printing is also reduced because some activities have changed since students now have devices. Previously, students may have used a worksheet activity to practice a skill, whereas now students can practice the same skill with an online game or interactive website.

We are not advocating you become a paperless classroom; sometimes paper is the right tool for the job. We are encouraging you, however, to think twice before you submit a printing job. Before printing, consider the following:

- Is this something students can access on their devices?
- Can you save time and resources by sharing it online rather than printing it?
- Do you need a printed version in order to assess the product?
- Does collecting a digital version make it easier to share to a wider audience?

If you decide to print, some procedural considerations must be made: You will need to determine the most efficient way for students to print, utilizing the least amount of learning time and offering the fewest opportunities for disruptions. As with all procedures, you will also need to spend some class time teaching your students and allowing them to practice the procedure. As you develop a printing procedure, you will need to take into account the following:

- Where to print (the physical location of printers at the school)
- When to print (when printers are available and when students are allowed to print)
- How to print (the technical how-to of connecting to a printer and releasing a print job)

If this gives you a headache, remember that collecting assignments digitally has gotten easier and easier. Printing remains a time-consuming, resource-intensive practice. Avoid printing when possible.

CLASSROOM RULES AND EXPECTATIONS

THE FIRST RULE OF CLASSROOM MANAGEMENT—clearly communicate classroom expectations around behavior—extends to the digital classroom as well.

CULTURE SETTING

SCHOOL

As you establish your expectations, begin with school-wide rules. Is there a Digital Citizenship Agreement (DCA) or Acceptable Use Policy (AUP) to which all students must agree? Does your school have a set of values or character traits tied into the curriculum? These can be the basis for your classroom expectations and conversations when misbehavior occurs.

CLASSROOM

You should also clearly communicate any specific classroom rules or expectations you have. You may want to consider using one of the ideas we share about creating an efficient work flow in your classroom to form the basis of your classroom expectations; for example, if an activator activity [see Activator: What Students Do When They Walk into the Room] becomes part of your daily routine, your expectation will be for students to always look for the activator and begin working when they walk into the classroom. It won't be long before all students are learning from the moment they arrive.

ONLY SET RULES YOU PLAN TO ENFORCE

When you run into a challenge in your 1:1 classroom—and you will—your first reaction might be to make a new rule to address it. But if you add a rule with each challenge, you will soon find you have too many rules you cannot realistically enforce. Similarly, do not make false threats; students can easily see through them. Say what you mean and follow through with consequences.

As you consider expectations for your classroom, think about the overall goal of your classroom: Using technology for learning. When challenges arise, rather than creating a new rule, relate the challenge back to your goal. Keep your expectations simple enough that any student can quickly state them when asked.

AVOID TEACHER TECHNO PANIC

In some ways, the digital world can magnify our mistakes or bad behavior in a way not possible in the analog world. If you made a mistake when you were in your teens, a handful of people might have known about it. You learned from it, and then you probably forgot about it. Today, a mistake can easily be captured as a photo or video and shared with thousands, making it difficult to forget.

Get rid of techno panic by considering the analog equivalent of behavior issues.

While technology can create real problems that need to be addressed with students, the potential exists for educators to magnify misbehavior that occurs on or with a digital device. If a student is chatting online with another student during class, for instance, teachers may overreact with "techno panic" and want to ban every form of digital communication from the classroom. The actual problem is a distracted student communicating with another student, the digital equivalent of passing a note or whispering in an analog classroom.

Get rid of techno panic by considering the analog equivalent of behavior issues. Chances are that the same techniques used in the analog classroom will work in your digital one as well.

BATTERY-LIFE MANAGEMENT

In a 1:1 program where devices go home with students each day, they can be charged at the students' homes or at school. Either way, the responsibility for charging them should always belong to the students.

NO CHARGING AT SCHOOL

Many successful laptop and tablet programs have rules restricting students from bringing the charger cable to school. Students are expected to come to school with a fully charged device each day, and to manage the battery life to ensure the device functions through the last class. For this to happen, two conditions must exist: First, the device must actually have a battery life capable of lasting through the school day. Second, teachers must allow students to experience the natural consequences when the device runs out of battery power: The student will not have a device to use. Students want to use their devices, and they will manage their batteries well if we give them the responsibility and maintain high expectations for them.

CHARGING AT SCHOOL ALLOWED

If students are allowed to charge their devices at school, they are less likely to come to school prepared, creating more instances of devices that need to be charged during the day. If this is the case at your school, make sure students understand it is their responsibility to plug in their device quickly, quietly, and at the appropriate time. The teacher's only responsibility is to clearly communicate where outlets are located. Students should be able to plug in when needed without drawing attention to themselves or distracting other students.

CHARGING IN A SHARED-DEVICE CLASSROOM

Sharing devices creates a unique challenge related to battery life. Nothing is worse for a student than discovering the inconsiderate person who used the device previously did not reconnect it properly to the power cable. Suffering the consequences of someone else's inattention to detail is never fun.

If you teach in a shared-device classroom and devices are charged in the room, you will need to take the team approach and preach that it is everyone's responsibility to ensure devices are connected properly when they are put away so they are charged for the next person. Assigning a specific device to each student, rather than students using random devices each class, can increase the feeling of ownership, care, and responsibility a student has toward the device. Even so, you will want to check the devices before you dismiss the class. Better yet, give the responsibility of checking the devices to a couple of responsible students. They can check the whole set of devices at the end of each class and confirm with you everything is connected properly, and then you can dismiss the class.

CARING FOR THE DEVICE

Whether devices are student-owned or school-owned, whether they travel with students or stay in a specific classroom, a culture of responsible care for the equipment should be established. Damage to devices results in expensive repairs or replacement costs, and being without the devices can cause huge disruptions to learning. The teacher of a well-managed classroom establishes a culture of responsible use and communicates clear guidelines about basic processes regarding transport of devices. Below are a few things to think about as you establish your classroom rules and procedures.

ACCESSING DEVICES

Students bringing devices to class need to know where to put them. Do they put them on their desks, under their desks, or in a storage area? If devices are stored in your classroom, you will need to establish how students retrieve devices and put them away again.

TRANSPORTING DEVICES

Hopefully your school has established guidelines for carrying devices because getting reinforcement from all teachers helps students remember them. Simple guidelines like "always use two hands" work well. With laptops, instructing students to close the lid and zip the case (if there is one) is a better practice than allowing students to move about the class with the laptop open.

WHAT *NOT* TO DO WITH A DEVICE

As much as students need guidelines for proper use, they also need instructions about what to avoid to prevent costly damages.

LIQUIDS

Students should keep their digital devices away from liquids. Even a tiny drop of water can cause hundreds of dollars of damage to a device. Many teachers allow water bottles in the classroom, but they should be kept on the ground so they are never on the same surface as the devices.

SAFE SURFACES

Students should put their devices squarely on a table or flat surface, not hanging over the edge. Likewise, devices should never be placed, as I like to say, "in places where feet and bums go." This keeps devices on elevated surfaces (desks, tables, and counters) and not on stairs, chairs, benches, and the floor, which pose significant danger to devices being sat on or stepped on.

BE PREPARED TO LEARN

Create your own "be prepared to learn" habit by identifying and reinforcing the most important things necessary for students to be fully ready to use their devices for learning. That may mean that students from one 1:1 laptop school are responsible every day for having the

laptop available and ready to go, a fully charged battery, and earbuds in the laptop case. If any of those are missing, learning time is lost.

The most important things in your classroom will depend on your specific situation. Perhaps you have shared devices so students need to log out of their accounts before leaving class or maybe students need to check that their devices are charging correctly before leaving the classroom. Whatever your situation, determine what is essential for students to be ready to learn every day with technology.

No Audio Zone

Some 1:1 classrooms are considered "no audio zones" because students must use headphones when listening to video or audio independently. We are not advocating students be allowed to listen to music or watch YouTube videos when they should be focused on writing an essay. But when students need to listen to audio or watch a video as part of a research assignment, this allows them to be respectful of other students' learning by not distracting them.

Posters

Once you have identified your main processes and procedures, create posters to "advertise" them in your classroom. These serve as visual reminders of your expectations, and you can refer to them when correcting behavior. Soon, your "ad campaign" will pay off as procedures develop into routines, and students monitor and correct themselves and one another.

We've included an example set of ad campaign posters here that you can download and use in your own classroom:

- Be Prepared to Learn
- Plug In
- Think before You Post
- Ask Three before Me
- Liquid is the #1 Enemy of Devices

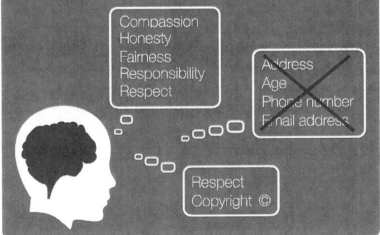

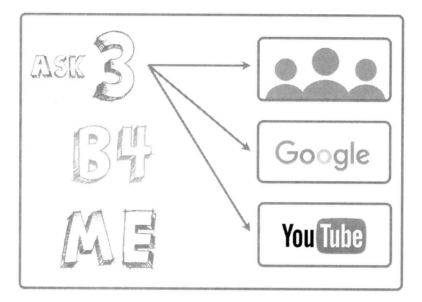

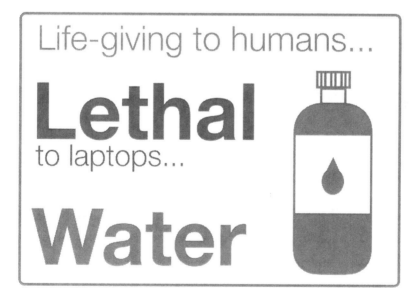

DOWNLOAD THESE POSTERS AT
EDTECH.TEAM/DOWNLOADPOSTERS

Digital Citizenship

Teaching students to be good citizens is not new. We were doing this long before we had any technology devices in our classrooms. Today we have the responsibility to help students become good citizens both offline and online. Hence, it is important you address in your device-rich classroom what it means to behave well online. This is the simple definition of digital citizenship.

As 1:1 programs expand around the world, educators need to understand the various categories of digital citizenship and integrate them across the curriculum. Early on, schools treated digital citizenship as a special event. We have found that treating the topic as a one-off special event removes it from context and does not give it the attention it deserves. Digital citizenship must be part of our students' daily lives at school and at home.

Fortunately, high-quality and free digital citizenship resources and lesson plans are available for teachers. Common Sense Education has a comprehensive K–12 scope and sequence of lessons and other resources including lesson plans and student-directed online tools. Additionally, they provide assessments to engage students in topics on self-image and identity, relationships and communication, digital footprint and reputation, cyberbullying and digital drama, information literacy, Internet safety, privacy and security, and creative credit and copyright.

Look at Common Sense Education's digital citizenship curriculum on their website (commonsensemedia.org) to find lessons available for your grade level. While each lesson is meant to be a stand-alone

Digital citizenship must be part of our students' daily lives at school and at home.

forty-five minute lesson, you may decide you need just one piece of one lesson to integrate into another project you are doing. As such, do not feel as though you need to use the lesson plans exactly as written. Use these resources in the way that makes sense for your classroom. If we all take some responsibility for helping students become good digital citizens, our students will be on their way to using technology ethically and responsibly.

WHAT TO DO WHEN YOU COME ACROSS AN INAPPROPRIATE WEBSITE

Most schools have Internet filters in place to help protect our youngest learners from accidentally viewing inappropriate material. Even with numerous filters and boundaries, inappropriate websites can still sneak through these safety measures. Teachers need to be prepared for this and train their students to handle these situations. In our experience, simply having an age-appropriate conversation with students is the best method for ensuring students know what to do when this occurs. One suggestion is to instruct students to close the tab of the inappropriate site and tell the teacher. The teacher can then look at the search history and, potentially, determine how the student arrived there. This simple rule works well in elementary schools, but likely needs to be modified for middle schools and beyond.

BOOT CAMP

As you begin using 1:1 devices in your classroom, you will want to spend time teaching your students about the technology and expectations for using it. Spending time at the beginning will be worth it because students will have the skills and resources needed to use their devices in responsible ways.

Many schools conduct a "boot camp" to kick off a new 1:1 device program and require students to complete the camp before they are allowed to take home their device. An example of this kind of program is a school that takes two full days at the beginning of the year to kick off its 1:1 laptop program. Students do a variety of activities designed to familiarize themselves with their devices and the program. Topics include digital citizenship, laptop care, productivity and organization, and using the laptop in a healthy way. If your school offers a boot camp, make sure you are familiar with what students learn so you can reinforce those skills in your classroom throughout the school year. You can follow up with a mini boot camp in your classroom so students know classroom-specific rules and expectations.

If your school does not hold a boot camp for students, you can still conduct one in your own classroom. Depending on your schedule and how much time you have with students, you can customize activities to fit within your parameters. Topics you might consider covering include the following:

- *Acceptable Use Policy / Digital Citizenship Agreement*—If your school has an AUP or something similar, spend some time reading it together with students. Help them understand what they are signing and agreeing to in exchange for using a school device.

- *Privacy and Security*—Help students set strong passwords for their devices and accounts. Teach them what information they should always keep private (last name and home address, for example) when they are posting online.

- *Laptop Care and Handling*—Teach students how to be responsible users and take care of their devices. Topics could include charging, proper storage, use of cases, and where to safely use the devices.

- *How to Use the Device*—Contrary to popular belief, students are not born knowing how to use technology. They learn by doing. Teach students how to use the device, both the hardware and the software. Design a few activities to introduce students to apps/programs on their devices.

- *Digital Citizenship*—While a boot camp is not the only time digital citizenship should be addressed, it is a great time to kick off the school year on the right track. Teach students what good digital citizenship means and consider asking them to take a digital citizenship pledge. Or combine the main ideas of digital citizenship with the most important classroom expectations and have students take a pledge to uphold both.

Involve parents in the boot camp process. Have students teach their parents something they learned during boot camp and, if your students will take their devices home, help families set expectations for their use at home. One way to do this is to develop a list of agreements parents and students can modify for their use. For example:

- Agree the laptop does not belong to the student but to the school, and its main purpose is for academic learning.

- Agree on what the laptop should—and should not—be used for outside of its main purpose. Consider whether you will allow the student to play games, socialize, use social networks, etc.

- Agree on where the laptop will be charged each night. Consider the location, time, and how this will fit into the student's evening routine (e.g., after brushing teeth).

- Agree on where and when the laptop can be used at home. Consider private vs. public spaces, balance between screen time and face time, and establishing an "Internet curfew." Be mindful of dangerous locations for laptops.

- Agree on what happens during homework time. Consider setting expectations about a specific location for doing homework and what types of apps and services should be turned off. Consider how "break time" might look different than "homework time."

- Agree to keep an open and honest dialogue about the student's digital life. Consider setting expectations about how to deal with cyberbullying and what to do if students come across inappropriate websites.

- Agree to make future adjustments to these agreements or create new agreements as needed.

Common Sense Education also has a Family Media Agreement you can share with parents as a way to encourage open conversation with their children about expectations at home.

DEALING WITH DISTRACTION

TEACH STUDENTS ABOUT MULTITASKING

Because we are constantly doing many things at once, it is easy to believe multitasking is a reality. Imagine you are making dinner and having a conversation with a family member. Seems easy, right? But imagine you are making a meal you have never made before and reading the recipe to make sure to follow the right order. Now having a conversation with your family member isn't so easy, is it? The difference between these two scenarios is the attention required to perform the task. If you are making a meal you know well, you can give some

Brain research concludes "multitasking, when it comes to paying attention, is a myth."

of your attention to your family. But if you need to pay full attention to the recipe, it is more difficult to share your attention with anything else.

This is not just anecdotal. Brain research concludes "multitasking, when it comes to paying attention, is a myth."[1] We may think we are multitasking, but we are actually doing only one thing, shifting our attention to something else, and then shifting our attention back to the original task. This shifting of attention requires effort from our brains; therefore, we take longer to complete a task, and we make more mistakes.

How does this apply to the device-rich classroom? Students believe they can multitask, but they cannot. They think they can have multiple apps and tabs open and remain focused on a class project. But every time they respond to the chat window ding or switch over to a game or make a few edits on a movie they are making, they are shifting their attention away from the task on which they should be focused.

Many students will also say music helps them focus on homework tasks, but most research does not corroborate this belief. While music itself is not bad and can even set the stage for a period of history you are studying or set a positive environment in your classroom, listening to music can distract students from paying attention to a learning task. Since it appears the lyrics are what pull students' attention away from the task, if students want to experiment with listening to music and focusing on something, encourage them to try listening to classical music and see if it makes a difference.

Understanding that multitasking is a myth, let us consider how to help students manage their own distractions. Have a conversation with your students about the myth and how easy it is to be distracted. Encourage students to be reflective, objective, and honest about their attempts to multitask in the classroom or at home, and share your own

---

1 John Medina, *Brain Rules* (Pear Press, 2014).

challenges with multitasking. Finally, share the research about multitasking and work with your students to minimize the distractions stealing their attention.

MANAGE DISTRACTION

Technology is a powerful tool for learning, creativity, productivity, and communication. But along with this power comes a great deal of potential distraction, a shift teachers and students alike are dealing with. As technology makes staying connected and completing multiple tasks easier, it also makes distractions prevalent. Managing these distractions is a skill students need as they move toward university and into the work place. How can we support and guide our students to stay focused while using these powerful tools?

ENGAGE STUDENTS IN HELPING THEMSELVES

The most valuable thing a teacher can do is empower students to keep themselves focused. Discuss digital distraction openly at school and ask students to collaborate to come up with strategies they can use to help themselves. Strategies may include rules students make for themselves such as *I can only play my favorite computer game at home after my homework is finished and I've exercised for thirty minutes.* Other strategies may include digital tools limiting a student's access to certain websites after a certain amount of time. Whether the strategies are digital or not, have students test out various strategies and report back after a certain time period. Different strategies work for different students, and they are much more likely to minimize distraction if they choose the solutions rather than having a rule imposed upon them by parents or teachers.

CLOSE UNNECESSARY APPS AND TABS

Since it is difficult for students to ignore distractions like pop-up chat messages or an open game, give them sixty seconds at the beginning of class to close all open apps and tabs on their devices except for what is needed for class. This allows you to spend time on the learning target rather than on disciplining a student who got off-task. Plus, students are learning a good habit they can use personally when they need to focus.

DISCONNECT FROM WI-FI

If your students' task doesn't require Wi-Fi, ask them to turn it off on their devices. This will limit interruptions and make it more difficult for them to quickly check email or chat. Can students secretly turn it back on? Of course, and some will. But many of your students will appreciate the modeling of a focusing behavior and might use this strategy on their own when they need to accomplish other tasks.

LOCK STUDENTS TO AN APP

Many computer lab arrangements use software to allow the teacher to take control of student devices and may even give teachers the ability to lock students to a specific app or website. Taking this sort of action certainly minimizes distraction, but it also takes autonomy away from your students. While this may be an appropriate strategy, depending on the age of your students and the maturity of your 1:1 program, eventually it is best to give more autonomy to students so they have the opportunity to develop good digital citizenship skills.

MAKE YOUR LESSON ENGAGING

Students are much less likely to get distracted if the project on which they are working is intellectually engaging. If students are bored, it is hard to blame them for taking a second to check email or browse Facebook. Even the most responsible and respectful adults can fall prey to boredom. Just think about the last faculty meeting you attended!

TEACHING TIPS
AND STRATEGIES

THE PREVIOUS CHAPTERS OUTLINED PROCEDURES, PROCESSES, RULES, AND EXPECTATIONS THAT YOU CAN WEAVE INTO THE DAILY CLASSROOM ROUTINE. In this chapter, we will offer some tips and strategies that you can apply to your teaching practice as you plan learning activities. Some of these strategies may become regular procedures in your classroom and others may be useful for a specific activity. Either way, we hope these tips will help you manage your classroom for maximum learning.

ROOM ARRANGEMENT

Effective teachers arrange their classrooms to maximize learning, varying the classroom arrangement based on the type of learning task assigned. When you are explaining a new procedure and need all students facing forward with eyes on you, the best arrangement is desks set up in rows and columns. That said, different arrangements may better facilitate other types of learning tasks.

Teacher mobility is another thing to consider when arranging the classroom. Most teachers learn about the power of proximity during teacher training and understand the closer they are to a student, the less likely she is to get off task. Because teachers need to be able to assist each student, the teacher will want to make sure any arrangement provides a clear and short path to each student.

A third consideration when arranging the classroom is how to monitor on-task behavior. Before digital devices were used, a teacher could quickly scan the room from the front and have a pretty good account of how many students were on task. But in a 1:1 classroom there is a lot more uncertainty. Today, teachers must arrange their rooms so they can monitor all screens while enabling maximum productivity.

A variety of popular classroom layouts are outlined below.

TEACHER AT THE FRONT

Arranging the classroom so you are at the front is best when you need to communicate direct instruction or specific information to students. This arrangement works well in small doses and can be alternated with you being at the back of the room if your lesson alternates between direct instruction and practice. In this arrangement, devices most likely should be closed so the teacher is not in a constant tug-of-war for students' attention.

TEACHER IN THE CENTER

Teachers may prefer to be in the center of the room with students facing away, lined up as spokes on a wheel. This arrangement is popular when students are working independently and proves especially useful when the teacher needs to conference with individual students. The arrangement also allows the teacher to glance up and around to

Teachers must arrange their rooms so they can monitor all screens while enabling maximum productivity.

quickly check screens. Plus, off-task behavior is decreased because students are faced away from the teacher and unaware of his attention at any given time. This arrangement can also be modified to use with pairs of students.

TEACHER AT THE BACK

Placing the teacher at the back of the room, with desks arranged in columns and rows, works similarly well for monitoring purposes and is especially useful when switching back and forth from direct instruction to independent work multiple times during the same class period. The teacher simply moves to the front to present and moves to the back during student practice time.

PODS AND PAIRS

Arranging students in pairs or small groups clustered around the room is great for co-creation, discussion, group problem-solving, and any other type of student collaboration. If utilizing pairs all facing the same direction, the teacher can rotate to the back of the room to quickly scan the screens. Pods of three or four students will require they face all directions, so the teacher must continually move about the room to monitor screens. One trick to employ is to limit a pair of students to just one device, potentially increasing the communication, collaboration, and on-task behavior since students cannot drift off into their own screens.

STUDENTS RANDOMLY SCATTERED

Increasingly, classrooms are being designed for and outfitted with more flexible furniture allowing for a variety of classroom layouts. A number of items are currently available to allow for numerous classroom arrangements and the individual comfort of each student: desks and tables that can be separated for individual work or joined together for group work, height-adjustable desks allowing students to stand, and soft pillows or bean bags so students can stretch out on the floor. Allowing students a choice of where to sit (or stand) during independent work time is a common practice. While this environment creates a lot of flexibility for students, teachers must always consider how they will monitor on-task behavior. If all the students choose to migrate to areas where their screens are not readily viewable to the teacher (e.g., sitting with their backs against the wall), she may want to revisit using this random arrangement.

UNMOVABLE DESKS

In some classrooms, furniture is difficult or impossible to move. Large lab benches in a science classroom, for example, likely cannot be moved. If you have this situation, you might be wondering about an arrangement conducive to learning with devices. Since you don't have as much flexibility as other classrooms, you may have to get creative. Accept that you cannot try all of the options listed here and focus on the things you can control.

TEACHER AT THE TEACHER DESK

The "teacher at the teacher desk" arrangement works great—when students are not present in the classroom! Teaching today is active and requires teachers get out from behind their desks and be engaged with the students. The teacher's role is continuing to shift away from "content expert" to the "guide on the side" model. Teaching requires teachers to be active and mobile, and able to continuously monitor the communication and collaboration happening in the room. If a teacher is behind his desk, he is too far away from most students to observe, prod, redirect, ask questions, guide, prompt, encourage, or challenge students. If this is upsetting, I apologize—and encourage you to purchase some comfortable shoes!

Seating Assignments

Should a teacher assign seats or let students choose their own seats? Many beginning teachers wrestle with this question, and there is a wide spectrum in practice from teachers who always assign seats to teachers who never do. While you will eventually settle into what is most comfortable for you, here are a few points to consider:

Arrangement Trumps Assignment

Because seating arrangements can be matched with specific classroom tasks to maximize learning, classroom arrangement is more important than individual seat assignment.

Assign Seats on the First Day

Assigning seats on the first day of class saves time and can have a calming effect on students. It eliminates one of the many "unknowns" of that first day and can decrease anxiety for students who find it stressful to locate a seat (and their place within a social group). A teacher can always move toward unassigned seating once procedures are common knowledge and stronger student relationships have been built.

Partnering Students

Partnering high-performing students with students who could use some mentoring is often used to determine seating assignments. In a device-rich classroom, teachers can partner a "tech guru" student with a less tech-savvy student to support the skill development of the less-savvy student. This strategy also comes in handy when a new student joins the class mid-year. A tech guru partnered with a new student can help the new student quickly get up to speed on basic tech processes in the classroom.

Be Organized

Most technologies are created to make our lives easier and more efficient, but the variety of choices they offer can sometimes complicate things; therefore, organization in the classroom is more important than ever. Teachers and students should be focused on learning, not on how to figure things out or find information. We have suggested various strategies for workflow and general organization. Choose what works for you to create a consistent workflow to manage and use the devices in your classroom and communicate those expectations and processes to your students. They will thank you for making it easier for them to focus on learning the content.

Be Ready When Class Begins

Get all of your technology ready for upcoming lessons before class begins. Mentally go through your lesson, open a new tab for each website you need, and open any files or apps you need open. Just as you prepare physical materials needed for a lesson, you must also prepare digital materials. One strategy we use while planning a lesson is to save all the necessary tabs as bookmarks. When it is time to teach the lesson, we can open up all bookmarks in a window and be ready to go.

Personalize the Learning

A 1:1 device classroom offers your learners an amazing opportunity to personalize their learning in a way not possible before. Because students do not all need to do the exact same thing at the same time, you can design classroom tasks at each student's level. If you think this sounds scary, you are not alone. Teachers who have embraced personalized learning say it feels like they have lost control. But we would argue they have actually freed students to learn as they need to learn and, as a result, have let students take back control of their learning.

You can try this in your classroom in a variety of ways. Perhaps the most familiar is to use the device to differentiate learning of a basic skill. If some students are struggling to learn a new math concept, for example, you can find an app or website to help develop the concept for those students. Other students can reinforce their knowledge with a different application activity.

At the other end of the spectrum is a completely personalized learning experience where students are choosing what they study, how they study, and how they report out their learning. Technology allows each student to select the method of learning best for him.

Whatever you decide about personalized learning, remember your devices give you and your students powerful and easy access to resources. This alone can significantly change what your classroom can look like.

CREATE ENGAGING LESSONS

You know the feeling you get when you are so absorbed in a task that you lose track of time? Psychologist Mihaly Csikszentmihalyi's (pronounced Me-High Chick-Sent-Me-High) calls this "Flow" and defines it as "a state in which people are so involved in an activity that nothing else seems to matter; the experience is so enjoyable that people will continue to do it even at great cost, for the sheer sake of doing it."[1] When students feel a sense of flow during their classroom activities,

> When students feel a sense of flow during their classroom activities, misbehavior is not an issue.

---

1 Mihaly Csikszentmihalyi, *Flow* (Harper & Row, 1990).

misbehavior is not an issue. Therefore, we believe the best strategy for reducing misbehavior in a device-rich classroom, or any other type of classroom, is to make every activity as engaging as you can. When students are engaged in your lessons, they are not misbehaving. Of all the strategies we share in this book, this is the best one.

Target Higher-Order Thinking

One way to accomplish this is for students to use technology for higher-order tasks (Bloom's Taxonomy). Ask students questions they cannot answer with a simple Google search—questions requiring students to analyze, evaluate, and create. Better yet, teach students to ask good questions requiring these skills themselves.

Use Technology for Creation

Another way to keep students engaged is to encourage them to create. Technology is a powerful tool for creators, making it easier than ever to create podcasts, music, graphics, magazine layouts, posters, movies, etc. What used to be the domain of professionals is now within the reach of educators and students. Be brave and encourage your kids to create more than just five-paragraph essays. Use the nearly infinite creative options of the digital devices in your classroom to engage your students.

Let Students Explore

In his book *Brain Rules*, Dr. John Medina states, "we are powerful and natural explorers." Technology opens a whole new level of things to explore. Let students explore new software, new ideas, and new ways to do things. Let them teach you what they find.

Don't Be Boring

Ultimately, creating engaging lessons with technology ensures you will not risk boring your students. Medina also notes that, "We don't pay attention to boring things." Alternatively, when we are paying attention, we are better able to learn something. According to Medina, the best way to gain and keep our students' attention is by using "messages that grab our attention" and "are connected to memory, interest, and awareness."

GIVE STUDENTS CHOICE

Another way to reduce classroom management issues surrounding technology is to give students some choice in their technology use. When students choose, they can connect to previous experiences and memories. One way to give students choice in their learning is to allow them to choose the tool—perhaps an app or piece of software they have used in the past with success. Another choice you might give students is in how they show their learning; for example, students could choose to make a video or give a live talk.

CONNECT TO PERSONAL INTERESTS

As much as possible, connect classroom activities to students' interests. They will pay attention when the topic involves something in which they are interested. Many educators are incorporating "twenty percent time" (also called "passion time" or "genius hour"), a certain amount of time in class devoted to student interests or passions. But you don't have to formalize it to that extent. Think about ways you can meet the learning standards in your classroom but also allow the freedom for students to explore their interests. You might just find your students are more engaged.

DEALING WITH TECH QUESTIONS

In classrooms worldwide, the teacher's role is shifting from content expert to facilitator of learning experiences. The explosion of information and increased access to information through the Internet accentuates this shift. Just as it is absurd to think a teacher should know every fact contained in a textbook, a teacher cannot be expected to know how to use every app or piece of software on student devices. Yet many teachers feel a sense of panic when students ask tech questions, and some feel that they are not up to the job if they cannot answer them. But this is simply not true. A master teacher with absolutely no tech skills can still be a master teacher in a connected classroom if they adhere to the following tips:

KNOW YOUR ROLE

You must remember that, as the teacher, your primary goals are to help your students to learn, to think critically and creatively, and to be problem solvers. Ultimately, you want your students to function without you. If you teach math, your job is not to solve equations; it is to help students learn to solve equations on their own. The same goes for tech questions in the classroom. You should not be trying to answer all the tech questions; you should be helping students solve those questions on their own. The best way to get comfortable with this is to simply tell your class you are a teacher, not a technology expert. Let them know you are there to help them learn to solve problems for themselves, but you are not going to give them the answers.

Although you do not have to be a technology expert in the classroom, you do not need to be a Luddite either. A common phrase heard in classrooms and in staff meetings when something goes wrong with the technology is, "I'm just not a tech person." Avoid this phrase at all costs, as it sends terrible messages to other teachers and students. It communicates that giving up is okay, or that some people cannot learn new things or understand technology. Today we are all tech people simply because we need to utilize current tools. We don't need to be computer programmers, but we do need to have the right attitude toward learning new things. A more productive way to deal with a technology failure or frustration in class is to ask your students for help. Doing so models the kind of positive attitude about learning new things that you expect from your students.

COACH AND GUIDE

Once you have given yourself permission not to know all the answers, coaching and guiding students toward solving their own problems becomes easier. You have been trained to question, paraphrase, and summarize. Helping students get unstuck is what master teachers do naturally. Ask students what they have already tried, what strategies they might try next, who else they could ask, and what search terms they have used. By simply asking questions and getting students to think critically, you can get students going in the right direction while at the same time developing resilient problem-solvers.

LET STUDENTS BE THE "TECHXPERTS"

Declaring to your class you are not the tech expert creates a void a number of students will be willing to jump in and fill. These "techxperts" won't be hard to find—likely they are already recognized by their peers. Your job is to empower them and honor them for their expertise. A little praise goes a long way and, by recognizing your techxperts, you can develop a team of students ready and willing to take on the tougher tech challenges when they arise.

SURVEY THE ROOM FOR TECHXPERTS

If for any reason the techxperts aren't easily recognized in your class, a simple survey of the students will allow you to quickly identify a support network for new projects, software, or apps you introduce for the first time. You could ask students to create a podcast using GarageBand, or ask them to respond with a show of hands to the following questions:

- How many of you have used GarageBand before today?

- How many of you consider yourself GarageBand experts and would be willing to help others who run into technical difficulties?

Then, have your students look around the room so they know who can help. You can also develop different questions, of course, but these allow the teacher to quickly gauge the class's level of prior experience and identify the most knowledgeable students in the room.

Another way you might identify your techxperts is to post a list of the students who have indicated some expertise. This can be posted in the classroom, digitally on the class website, or in your LMS and might change from project to project depending on the tool being used. Some students might be techxperts in video creation while others are familiar with only the basic use of the device. Post multiple lists and then direct students to get help from those listed.

REPEAT THE MANTRA "ASK THREE BEFORE ME"

If you follow the tips above, you will be well on your way to creating a climate of support conducive to learning. One last step is to adopt the mantra Ask Three before Me and post it for all to see. Ask Three before Me requires students to ask three others—specifically Google, YouTube, and a peer—for assistance before asking you for assistance. Very likely, the answer can be found through an Internet search and, quite possibly, a step-by-step video on YouTube. If not, perhaps a peer can help. One of the best things we can do is give students the responsibility and opportunity to solve authentic problems. Adopting the "ask three before me" mantra gives students authentic learning opportunities and reiterates the teacher is not a tech expert. By the time a student brings you a question, they should be able to describe what they have already tried. At this point, you can slide into the "coaching and guiding" described previously and assist the student in developing a new strategy for finding the answer.

ENCOURAGE ORGANIZATION

Just as giving students time at the beginning of class to get ready to learn is important, it is equally important to give students time at the

> One of the best things we can do is give students the responsibility and opportunity to solve authentic problems.

end of a class to organize themselves and get ready to transition to the next activity. Building in time for closing the laptop, zipping the laptop bag, putting the device away in the correct location, and ensuring a device is charging will build good habits. Eventually, students will need less time to get ready to transition, and these things will happen routinely.

MANAGING PROJECTS

When teachers assign larger projects, whether technology related or not, some students will struggle with the organizational and goal-setting skills needed to be successful. Effective teachers have been scaffolding these skills long before devices entered our classrooms, and with the introduction of technology, the same scaffolding is needed. Students will need support to understand exactly what they are to complete and to set achievable goals.

HAVE CLEAR EXPECTATIONS

Giving clear expectations about what is required for the task is especially important when assigning a technology project; for example, if you want students to work on video production skills, rather than simply saying, "make a video about what you learned," give more details. Without fully understanding the expectations, students may film a ten-minute video—more than they can reasonably handle. Give students a time limit and insist they create a storyboard before they are allowed to film to make sure their ideas can be achieved in the allotted time.

Help Students Set Realistic Goals

When students begin a technology project, they are often unrealistic about what they can achieve within the time limit given. If students have ninety minutes to create something, for example, they may choose a topic needing weeks of time to complete. Help your students set realistic goals about what they can achieve in those ninety minutes. Both you and the students will avoid disappointment, and your students will learn to set their own goals with future projects.

Assign Roles

Assigning roles to students working on a task or project is a common strategy used by many teachers and can work well with devices, too. If the task students are working on does not require every student to be on a device, assign one student the role of using the device while others take different roles. Perhaps students are recording a science experiment. One student can record what is happening and another student can share the video with the other students. If a written record of a group discussion is needed, one student can be the notetaker. If students are interacting with an online activity, it might make sense for two students to be on one device to encourage conversation between the two students as they do the activity. Yet another iteration of this strategy is to assign multiple technology roles within the same group; for example, one student takes photos while another types up observations. Obviously, this strategy is highly dependent on the type of activity you are doing. The key is to analyze the task and think about what is needed. In some cases, a 2:1 or 3:1 strategy may be better than a 1:1.

Use a Timer for a Task

Using a timer to keep students on task is a strategy used by teachers long before we had digital devices in the classroom, but remains a tried-and-true strategy to use with devices, especially in classrooms where the teacher plans a variety of activities during the class. Timers help students and teachers stay on task and be ready to proceed when the time is up. Experiment with various timer tools to find the best one for you. In an iOS classroom, or if you have an iPhone, you can utilize Siri and quickly say to your iPhone or iPad, "set a timer for five minutes." There are also many online timers which can be displayed on the screen at the front of the room. If the screen is needed for student instructions or something else, timer-tab.com displays the remaining time in a small tab at the top of the screen while you display another tab.

DON'T LEAD STUDENTS THROUGH A LONG SERIES OF CLICKS

When your instructions for software include a series of steps students must follow, do not let students attempt to follow you click by click. *This does not work.* Keeping a group of twenty in the same place when going through multiple clicks is impossible. Some students will be lost after just a few clicks. When you try to help those students get caught up, others will get lost. Ask students to put their devices down and watch you go through all the steps. You will find at least half of the students can then proceed independently, and you can empower the students to ask each other for help. Once you have explained the big picture and shown them the individual steps, you can also give them written instructions or a video to watch individually. You are then free to walk around and support students who need extra help.

HAVE A SENSE OF HUMOR

While you might be wondering what a sense of humor has to do with technology, we think it is essential to a 1:1 device program. You will have challenges along the way, just as you had before devices— technical problems, lack of understanding of a new tool, a flopped lesson, or a discipline problem. We think the best way to handle these challenges is with some flexibility, forgiveness, and a sense of humor.

Mistakes will happen, but the right environment in the classroom allows everyone to learn from them and move on.

ENCOURAGE ONLINE SHARING

Your 1:1 device classroom connects students to the world in a way like never before. A benefit of this widespread connection is their ability to author and publish their work to the online world. While few may be paying attention to most student blogs or sites, it is still important to cultivate a culture of sharing and creating a positive digital footprint.

Encourage your students to publish both in-process and completed work in a variety of online spaces in order to build a positive digital presence and develop a deeper understanding of how they can collaborate, create, share, and communicate online. Through publishing, students will practice good digital citizenship and develop an increased understanding of responsible online behavior. Presenting their work online provides students with a real audience from whom they can continue to grow and learn.

Publishing student work online should be a key component of a 1:1 device program, but students should be aware once information is on the Internet, nothing can stop it from being replicated, shared, and distributed widely without their control—immediately and into the future. Additionally, teachers must emphasize certain pieces of information, such as passwords and private information, should never be shared. Consider creating student guidelines for online sharing like the ones on the following page, and post them in your classroom.

TEACH RESEARCH SKILLS

Technology puts powerful research tools at our fingertips, but just as they did with card catalogs and reader's guides, students need guidance to develop research skills. Don't assume they automatically know how to conduct efficient and effective research simply because they can Google something. Teach them how to research by using a research

STUDENT GUIDELINES FOR ONLINE SHARING

SHARING INFORMATION ONLINE ALLOWS US TO...

- practice creating work for an audience beyond the classroom walls
- connect and collaborate with peers and experts globally
- archive learning in one place and reflect on personal growth
- showcase our creativity and share our ideas

WHAT YOU POST ONLINE IS PERMANENT.

Use the following to help you decide what is appropriate to publish:

Think before you post. Ask yourself the following questions:

- Is this something I want the world to see?
- Would sharing this offend anyone?
- Would I want this to represent my abilities?

Treat other people the way you want to be treated. Ask yourself the following questions:

- Would I say this to someone in person?
- How would I feel if someone said this to me?

Do not share personal information. Keep your last name, address, phone number, and email address private.

Properly cite media used from another source. Ask yourself:

- Who is the original creator of this work?
- Do I have permission to use this work?

model you create or using a model like Big6. Big6 is a "process model of how people of all ages solve an information problem." For more information, visit the Big6 website (http://big6.com/pages/about/big6-skills-overview.php). Google also provides many resources, including ready-to-use lesson plans and activities, to help students develop better Google search skills.

ASK QUESTIONS THAT A SIMPLE GOOGLE SEARCH WON'T ANSWER

A 1:1 classroom environment may mean a shift in the kinds of questions you ask and assignments you give. Because this incredible resource—the Internet—is in the hands of your students, you have an opportunity to create assignments and projects to make the most of it. Ask questions students cannot answer with a Google search. Instead, ask questions requiring smart Google searches to find information for students to synthesize into new understanding. Similarly, rather than banning devices for your assessments, see if you can design the assessment to allow students to use their devices to show their knowledge and understanding of a topic.

CHOOSING AND USING TOOLS

EMBRACE ANALOG

While technology can enhance learning in many ways, teachers should not use it just to be using technology. Teachers should continue to embrace analog when appropriate. Is it easier for students to grab a scrap of paper for a quick brainstorm activity? If so, use that. Should students record themselves reviewing a book if they can easily share their review with a partner during class? The answer depends on the desired outcome. If sharing the book review with the wider school community is important, students should use technology. But if the goal is getting students to talk about books, perhaps simply sharing with one person in class serves the purpose. Think about the learning objective and choose a tool—analog or digital—to meet it.

Consider the following when deciding to use a digital or analog tool in your classroom:

1. *Efficiency*—Which is more time-efficient?
2. *Learning Impact*—Does technology make a greater impact on learning?
3. *Transferability*—Does learning a new technology give students a skill they need in the future?

NOTE-TAKING

Note-taking is an interesting activity to examine in the context of digital versus analog, but with a couple of disclaimers: First, while note-taking is not frequently used in elementary schools, it does have a place in middle and high schools. Second, as with all instructional strategies, overuse or over-reliance on one strategy can lead to diminishing returns, not to mention bored students.

There are times when note-taking is appropriate. A teacher might ask students to read a chapter of a science textbook and take notes as homework. Or he might tell students to take notes as he lectures on a social studies topic. But should students use a digital or analog note-taking method? Let's consider the following options:

1. *Analog*—Students use paper and pencil to take notes individually.
2. *Digital*—Students collaborate on a set of group notes using a Google Doc.
3. *Digital*—Students collaborate on a mind-map using MindMeister.

The chart on the opposite page will help you understand these analog and digital options in terms of efficiency, learning impact and transferability.

Taking time to evaluate the digital and analog options is a new responsibility for twenty-first-century teachers. Choosing the right tool requires that you consider many variables since all three of these note-taking methods have value for students.

SHARE THE PURPOSE OF THE TASK

As you consider the various technology tools and types of projects students can do with them, make sure you share with your students the reason you chose a particular tool. If you ask students to create a stop-motion video showing a scientific process, one learning objective is the science content. But another learning objective may be to develop students' video skills because this form of communication is important in the twenty-first century. Share this thinking with the students. Also, consider assessing all important learning objectives. In this science video example, if you only assess the science content, you might save time by choosing a different form for students to show their learning; however, if you believe creating a video is important, include a small part of the video-making process into your assessment of the project.

ASSIGN A TOOL TO DEVELOP EXPERTISE

Many tools are available for students to use to demonstrate their knowledge. You may elect to choose the tool for the students; for example, you assign students to use Apple Pages to design a poster. You might do this because it is the first time they are using this particular tool, and you want to make sure all students develop some expertise with it. For the next project, you might choose another tool they can learn. In the future, students will be able to choose from multiple tools with which they already have experience.

	Analog		Digital
	Individual notes using paper and pencil	*Group notes using a Google Doc*	*Mind-map using MindMeister*
Efficiency	Jotting notes by hand is quick, but many students can type more quickly than they can write.	Getting started is relatively quick. Additionally, more information will be captured as students divide and conquer.	Because mapping is likely less familiar and potentially requires learning new software, it will take longer to get started.
Learning Impact	Many argue physically writing something down may lead to better understanding and recall than typing. Additionally, without devices there is no digital distraction.	All students will have the same set of notes and equal access to the information. Likely, notes are more thorough than they would be on paper and could include links to additional information on the Internet.	Concept maps can visually show connections and groupings of ideas better than linear notes. Additionally, students must use higher-order thinking skills to create a map.
Transferability	People will continue to write on paper in the future, but this skill is still practiced in schools.	Digitally documenting information (including the use of hyperlinks, embedded videos, and images) and collaboratively creating meaning in an online space are skills students will definitely use in the future.	Making connections between topics and representing those ideas visually is a contemporary skill which also allows students to think about design elements—another skill relevant to their future.

Allow Students to Choose the Best Tool

A downside of choosing the tool for students is limiting their creativity and freedom. Allowing students to choose the tool they think can best show their learning lets them select one familiar to them. Alternatively, they can choose a tool they want to better understand. This choice gives students a sense of independence, helps them become tech literate, and allows them to show their learning in a creative way that makes sense to them.

Let Students Figure Out the Details

Teachers used to feel they needed to know everything about a tool before using it with students. Given the sheer number of tech tools available, this is simply no longer realistic. If we waited until we felt proficient with everything before we used it with students, we would rob them of the opportunity to learn new skills and teach themselves when they get stuck. [Refer to "Ask Three Before Me."]

Before you assign students a tech tool to use, you should be generally familiar with it. You'll want to understand its purpose and know whether the tool is a good choice for the learning target. Try the activity you are asking students to do to get a sense of how much time the assignment might take to complete it. But you do not need to know every single aspect of the tool; the students can figure out the details. This will give them experience with teaching themselves and getting unstuck—important twenty-first-century skills—and empower them to help others learn.

Do a Trial Run on a Student Device

Before students begin using a tool, make sure it works on their devices. Don't just test it on your device and assume it will work on theirs. Often student devices have different settings, different access rights, or even different operating systems, and a tool working on your device may not work on theirs. If you have planned your lessons far enough ahead, you could ask a student who finishes work early to do a quick compatibility test of the next day's lesson.

PARTNERING WITH PARENTS

ESTABLISHING FREQUENT COMMUNICATION WITH YOUR STUDENTS' PARENTS HELPS BUILD A PARTNERSHIP based on a common goal of student success. Most parents have not learned in a classroom with digital devices, so they may have a difficult time envisioning a current classroom. They may also have misconceptions about how and why digital devices are used in the classroom. One common misconception is students will always have their faces in a screen. Effective teachers will use a balance of analog and digital experiences for students, but you can understand why parents who have never seen digital classrooms in action might have misconceptions. Even more reason for educators to focus on communicating with parents. Good communication can give parents a glimpse into the value of using digital devices in the classroom. This also creates rapport and a common understanding needed for conversations if students break classroom rules regarding responsible use of digital tools.

COMMUNICATION TOOLS

NEWSLETTER

Elementary teachers have historically utilized weekly or monthly newsletters to communicate current units of study, information regarding special schedules, holidays, field trips, learning, and featured activities in class. What began as a printed document carried home in backpacks has evolved into emails, blog posts, or class websites, complete with photo galleries and video of student activity and achievement.

SOCIAL MEDIA

Individual teachers and entire school districts have more recently taken to social media to promote the creativity and learning going on in their schools. Twitter and Instagram hashtags can be harnessed by teachers to showcase student work, promote school spirit, and create a positive community atmosphere. To see how two schools are using hashtags, check out #leydenpride (Leyden High Schools, Illinois) and #sasedu (Singapore American School). Teachers, students, and parents also post a variety of school highlights to Instagram and Twitter. Before using social media, check with your school administration regarding rules governing posting photos of individual students or other privacy rules potentially impacting the use of these tools.

OPEN HOUSE

Many schools create opportunities for parents to visit their child's classroom and meet their child's teacher. Meeting face-to-face creates familiarity and helps to decrease potential future misunderstandings among teachers and parents. If digital devices and technology-learning opportunities are new to your community, an open house is an excellent way to promote the creative, engaging activities you will be providing to your students. If your school does not currently host an open house, consider initiating one just for your students.

COMMUNICATION STRATEGIES

WHY DIGITAL DEVICES?

As 1:1 classrooms become more prevalent, and access to digital devices becomes the norm in classrooms, educators are engaging in conversations about the benefits that these classroom set-ups provide. But your students' parents may not have a good understanding of these benefits. Whether your entire school is 1:1, or you are the only teacher piloting this type of environment, engaging parents in conversations around the value of 1:1 is important. A number of organizations have done significant work outlining the types of twenty-first-century skills (creativity, communication, collaboration, etc.) that are best developed using current tools. If you need to bolster your understanding, peruse the documentation provided by the following organizations:

- Partnership for 21st Century Learning (p21.org)
- International Society for Technology in Education (iste.org)
- Anytime Anywhere Learning Foundation (aalf.org)

SHARE CLASSROOM EXPECTATIONS

As you set up the procedures and expectations for technology in your classroom, share those expectations with parents. Sharing your expectations educates parents about the type of classroom their children are in. It also empowers parents to reinforce and set similar expectations at home.

SHARE ASSESSMENT DATA

If your school does not use an online gradebook system, consider putting your individual class gradebook online. Having an up-to-date online gradebook gives parents an understanding of where their

> Sharing your expectations ... empowers parents to reinforce and set similar expectations at home.

students are in their learning at all times. If you do put your gradebook online, you may want to communicate a few expectations to parents and students. Parents and students often expect an immediate response to an email, so communicate your typical response time so parents don't become frustrated. Also, encourage parents to speak to their child first if they find an issue in the gradebook.

Share Classroom Activities

If parents are unfamiliar with a 1:1 device program, they may have some concerns about how the devices are being used in the classroom or misconceptions about how devices are used with their children. They may, for example, view devices as "babysitters" to keep children occupied. Parents may also assume because devices are in the classroom, students are using them one hundred percent of the time. Of course, in an effective teacher's classroom, neither of these statements is true.

Because parents may not see the benefits of having a device in the classroom for learning, it is important you have open communication with them about the amount of time students are spending on devices and the kinds of activities in which students are engaged. You will be responsible for explaining to parents that students are not on a device all day at school.

To combat the notion of a device being a babysitter, be clear with parents about the kinds of activities students will do with their devices. Focus on the creation of content, not just the consumption. Show how students will be interacting with others while using the devices. As the school year progresses, share with parents the products their students make. Parents will soon see the device can be a powerful creation tool.

PARENT HANDOFF

Depending on the age of your students and your school policy, your students may be allowed to take their devices home with them. If this is the case for your students, and your school 1:1 program does not include a formal parent handoff activity, you might consider some form of parent handoff for your classes.

A parent handoff allows you to be very clear with parents and students about who is in charge of the device at home. This process empowers parents to have a conversation about device use at home and set expectations.

As mentioned in the section on boot camp, a parent hand-off process can include some prompts to facilitate a discussion between parents and children regarding device use at home. (See the Common Sense Education Family Media Agreement[1] for some ideas.) You could try the following prompts:

- Where can the device be used?
- When is it off limits?
- Where should it be charged?

These guidelines and rules should be discussed and agreed upon by child and parent. Plus, a parent handoff process will make it clear to students that parents are in charge of the device at home. While this may seem intuitive to you, many parents and students need to be reminded of this. You may even have both parents and child sign a statement that establishes who is in charge at school and at home.

---

1 https://www.commonsensemedia.org/sites/default/files/uploads/pdfs/phase3_fma_all_grades.pdf

Parent handoff activities can take many different forms depending on your context. If it is feasible, you could have parents come to school in person with their child. You can facilitate a conversation about use at home and have a formal "ceremony" where you hand the device to the parent signifying the parent is in charge. Perhaps this can be part of a more formal activity at your school, like an open house.

If bringing parents to school is not realistic, this activity can take place at home facilitated by a handout you provide. Students and parents can discuss the expectations for using the device at home. You could track this by asking parents to sign a form verifying they did it or have students take a photo with their parent showing the filled-out form.

PARTING WORDS

DON'T BE AFRAID. When you think of people who are "good with technology," you may assume they know more than you do or have an innate skill to use technology. In our experience helping students and teachers use technology for learning, we have come to the conclusion this assumption is false. Some students and teachers of all ages easily learn new technology tools and navigate issues in a calm manner, but they are not inherently better at using technology than others. They just have a different attitude. They are not afraid to push buttons and try new things. They have an open mind when it comes to clicking through a new tool. They are explorers in a new world and do not need a manual or special workshop to dive in and try something new. Having the right attitude is the single most important trait—and best strategy—for navigating, progressing, and learning in a connected classroom.

> Having the right attitude is the single most important trait for navigating, progressing, and learning in a connected classroom.

KEEP LEARNING

As you create an effective and efficient device-rich classroom, remember to keep learning about using in-class technology. Just as we become better teachers by reflecting on our craft and collaborating with others, we become better users of technology for learning by doing the same thing. Seek help when you need it. Join a professional organization. Attend professional-learning events that are focused on technology. Connect with people online. Find mentors in your school with whom you can share ideas, successes, and failures. Create a support network for yourself, and keep learning!

Resources

ISTE Standards

The internationally recognized ISTE Standards (iste.org) provide "clear guidelines for the skills, knowledge, and approaches [students] need to succeed in the digital age." Read through the standards to get a sense of what a current 1:1 classroom can look and feel like. Standards are published for students, teachers, administrators, coaches, and computer science educators. We have listed the standards for students and teachers because we believe these can set the stage for a successful 1:1 device program.

ISTE Standards for Students (2016)

1. Empowered Learner
2. Digital Citizen
3. Knowledge Constructor
4. Innovative Designer
5. Computational Thinker
6. Creative Communicator
7. Global Collaborator

ISTE Standards for Teachers (2008)

1. Facilitate and inspire student learning and creativity
2. Design and develop digital-age learning experiences and assessments
3. Model digital-age work and learning
4. Promote and model digital citizenship and responsibility
5. Engage in professional growth and leadership

Common Sense

Common Sense Education (commonsensemedia.org) provides free, high- quality resources for teachers and parents with the goal of helping students use technology responsibly both at school and at home. The following resources relate to the content in this book:

Common Sense Education 1 to 1 Essentials Program
https://www.commonsensemedia.org/educators/1to1

This site provides a step-by-step guide to setting up a 1:1 device program. While you may not be responsible for the overall set up at your school, the resources contained in the guide will help you set up a 1:1 classroom.

Common Sense Education Family Media Agreement
https://www.commonsensemedia.org/sites/default/files/uploads/pdfs/phase3_fma_all_grades.pdf

You can use or modify this media agreement form to help guide parents through discussions with their children about the expectations for technology use at home.

Common Sense Education Digital Citizenship Curriculum
https://www.commonsensemedia.org/educators/scope-and-sequence

This digital citizenship scope and sequence provides an entire curriculum you can use with students to help them learn what good digital citizenship means.

Educational Origami

http://edorigami.wikispaces.com/

Educational Origami is a Wikispace devoted to twenty-first-century teaching and learning started by Andrew Churches. Andrew has done significant work in developing Acceptable Use Agreements (AUA) in schools. If your school is looking to create a new AUA, or make your current AUA more child friendly, check out http://edorigami.wikispaces.com/Digital+Citizen+AUA

Research Skills

Big6

http://big6.com/pages/about/big6-skills-overview.php

Big6 is one of many models for teaching students research skills in the age of information. The Big6 can help students break the giant task of research into manageable chunks. Visit the Big6 website for more information about the six stages of Big6.

Google Search Education

https://www.google.com/intl/en-us/insidesearch/searcheducation/

Google also provides many resources you can use to help students develop better Google search skills. Visit their site which includes ready-to-use lesson plans and activities.

Books

Brain Rules by John Medina
Flow by Mihaly Csikszentmihalyi

ACKNOWLEDGMENTS

We have had opportunities to work closely with numerous master educators who have continually adapted their classroom practice to the changing educational landscape. This book was only possible because of the rich experiences and amazing colleagues we have had at Singapore American School, International School of Prague, American School Foundation of Monterrey, Blaine School District #503, and Hinsdale South High School.

Thank you, also, to the educators in our extended personal-learning networks with and from whom we have had the opportunity to learn both in person and online. Your wisdom and thoughtfulness about learning have pushed us to become better teachers.

We would also like to acknowledge all of those students in our first years of teaching who gave us plenty of practice honing our classroom management skills. You'd be so proud of how far we've come.

MORE BOOKS FROM EDTECHTEAM PRESS
EDTECHTEAM.COM/BOOKS

THE HYPERDOC HANDBOOK
Digital Lesson Design Using Google Apps
By Lisa Highfill, Kelly Hilton, and Sarah Landis

The HyperDoc Handbook is a practical reference guide for all K–12 educators who want to transform their teaching into blended-learning environments. This bestselling book strikes the perfect balance between pedagogy and how-to tips while also providing ready-to-use lesson plans to get you started with HyperDocs right away.

INNOVATE WITH IPAD
Lessons to Transform Learning in the Classroom
By Karen Lirenman and Kristen Wideen

Written by two primary teachers, *Innovate with iPad* provides a complete selection of clearly explained, engaging, open-ended lessons to change the way you use iPad in the classroom. It features downloadable task cards, student-created examples, and extension ideas to use with your students. Whether you have access to one iPad for your entire class or one for each student, these lessons will help you transform learning in your classroom.

ASSESSMENT THAT MATTERS
Using Technology to Personalize Learning
By Kim Meldrum

In *Assessment That Matters,* Kim Meldrum explains the three types of assessment—assessment *as* learning, assessment *for* learning, and assessment *of* learning. Within her instruction on gathering rich assessment information, you'll find simple strategies and tips for using today's technology to allow students to demonstrate learning in creative and innovative ways.

THE SPACE
A Guide for Educators
By Rebecca Louise Hare and Robert Dillon

The Space takes the current conversation about reshaping school spaces to the next level. This book goes well beyond the ideas for learning-space design that focus on Pinterest-perfect classrooms and instead discusses real and practical ways to design learning spaces that support and drive learning.

A Learner's Paradise
How New Zealand Is Reimagining Education
By Richard Wells

What if teachers were truly trusted to run education? In *A Learner's Paradise*, Richard Wells describes New Zealand's forward-thinking education system in which teachers are empowered to do exactly that. With no prescribed curriculum, teachers and students work together to create individualized learning plans—all the way through the high school level. From this guidebook, you'll learn how New Zealand is reimagining education and setting an example for innovative educators, parents, and school districts everywhere to follow.

The Google Apps Guidebook
Lessons, Activities, and Projects Created by Students for Teachers
By Kern Kelley and the Tech Sherpas

The Google Apps Guidebook is filled with great ideas for the classroom from the voice of the students themselves. Each chapter introduces an engaging project that teaches students (and teachers) how to use one of Google's powerful tools. Projects are differentiated for a variety of age ranges and can be adapted for most content areas.

DIVE INTO INQUIRY

Amplify Learning and Empower Student Voice

By Trevor MacKenzie

Dive into Inquiry beautifully marries the voice and choice of inquiry with the structure and support required to optimize learning. With *Dive into Inquiry* you'll gain an understanding of how to best support your learners as they shift from a traditional learning model into the inquiry classroom where student agency is fostered and celebrated each and every day.

Sign up to learn more about new and upcoming books at bit.ly/edtechteambooks

WANT MORE CLASSROOM MANAGEMENT TIPS?

HERE ARE WAYS TO STAY CONNECTED:

HOST A WORKSHOP AT YOUR SCHOOL

Digital-Age Classroom Management—Design a classroom plan to address everything from procedures and routines to a technology boot camp to Digital Citizenship. (Full, or half-day workshop)

Private Label—Heather Dowd and Patrick Green can customize a workshop to fit your school's specific needs

TAKE THE ONLINE COURSE for Classroom Management in the Digital Age

ATTEND AN EDTECHTEAM SUMMIT featuring Google for Education in your area.

Learn more at EdTechTeam.com/books

To request a workshop or for more info contact
press@edtechteam.com

facebook.com/groups/CMDigitalAge | #CMDigitalAge | @CMDigitalAge

ABOUT THE AUTHORS

HEATHER DOWD is a teacher, education technology coach, science enthusiast, traveler, photographer, and most of all, a learner. She has worked as a physics teacher, instructional designer, and education technology coach in Japan, the United States, Mexico, and Singapore. She currently enjoys leading professional learning workshops to help teachers create engaging experiences for students. Teaching English with the JET program in Kumamoto, Japan inspired her to become a teacher, and the adventure hasn't stopped. Heather is a Google for Education Certified Innovator/Trainer, Apple Distinguished Educator, and a Common Sense Digital Citizenship Certified Educator who believes students should have access to current technology in order to be creative in ways that weren't possible when she was in school.

PATRICK GREEN is an Education Technology Coordinator and Site Director for the Global Online Academy for the Singapore American School. He dreams of a world where people no longer use the word "technology" and instead talk about and seamlessly integrate relevant tools into their learning practice. Patrick thrives in the diverse connections his career offers. He works enthusiastically with students, parents, teachers, and community stakeholders to help them meaningfully create, collaborate, communicate, and critically think.

Having taught in the Pacific Northwest, the Czech Republic, and now Singapore, Patrick is nearing his twentieth year as an educational leader. He continues to find his inspiration first and foremost as a learner. He is an Apple Distinguished Educator, Principal's Training Center Trainer, Google Certified Innovator, Google Education Trainer, Common Sense Digital Citizenship Certified Educator, and a YouTube Star Teacher.

CPSIA information can be obtained
at www.ICGtesting.com
Printed in the USA
LVOW10s0139210617
538826LV00009B/185/P